Why We Celebrate Chanukah

Written and Illustrated by Howard M. Kurtz

This book belongs to:

_____

Written and Illustrated by
Howard M. Kurtz

Copyright ©2011 by
Pigment & Hue, Inc.
www.pigmentandhue.com

ISBN: 978-1-60798-100-8

Printed in China

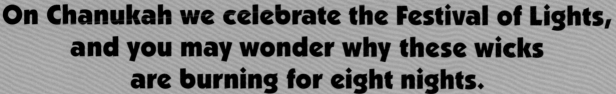

On Chanukah we celebrate the Festival of Lights, and you may wonder why these wicks are burning for eight nights.

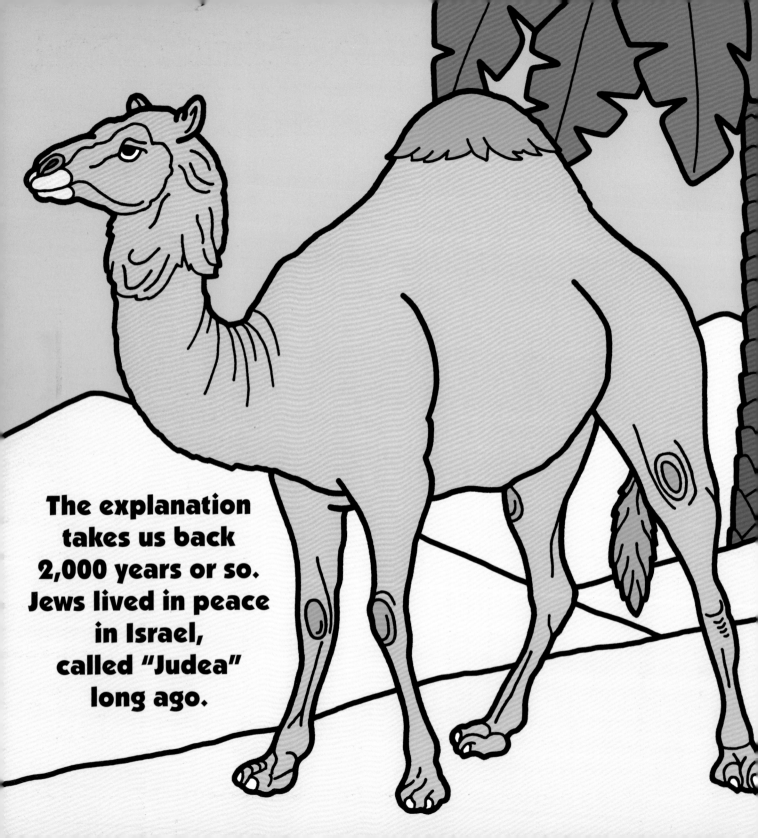

The explanation takes us back 2,000 years or so. Jews lived in peace in Israel, called "Judea" long ago.

The Temple
in Jerusalem
stood gleaming
white and tall,
and Jews could
worship freely;
no one bothered
them at all.

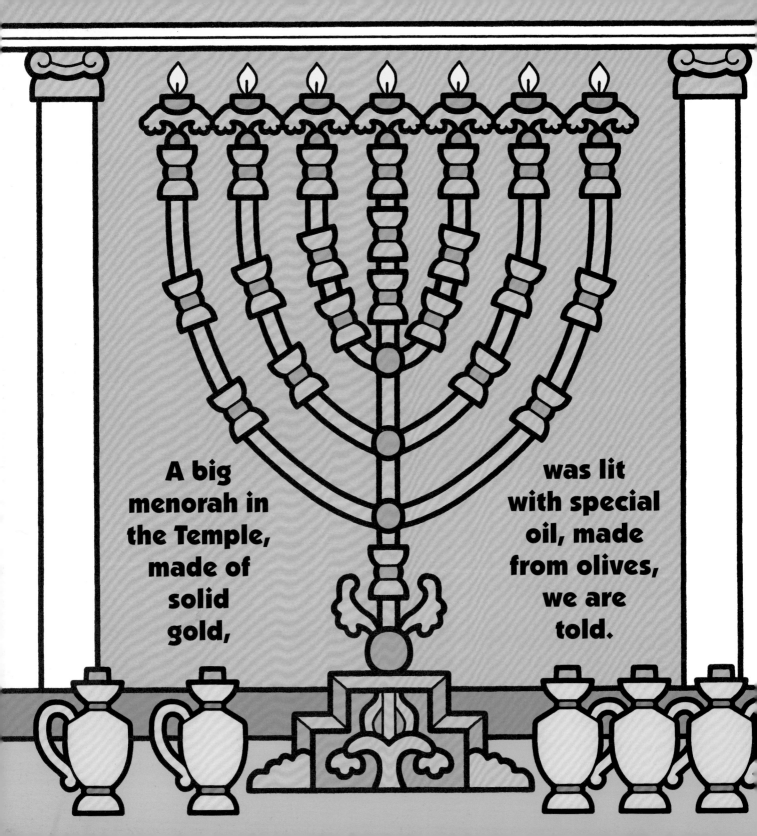

A big menorah in the Temple, made of solid gold,

was lit with special oil, made from olives, we are told.

Then one day, the Greek king Antiochus took a stand:
"All freedom of religion for the Jews will now be banned."

His soldiers marched right through the Temple, stealing what they could, with elephants destroying things of silver, gold and wood.

Upon the altar,
they put pigs,
which made that holy space

unclean and now not fit to be
a special prayer place.

"In front of this big statue," they said, "Jews must bow to Zeus."

The Jews did not know how they could endure such harsh abuse.

A man named Mattathias and his sons
then formed a plan:
"We'll leave our town of Modi'in
and fight this evil man!"

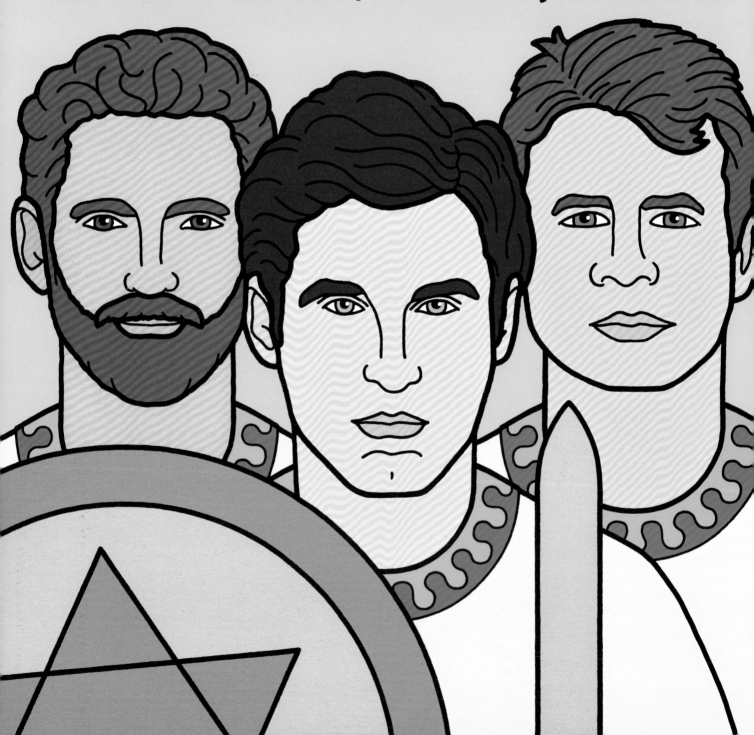

"With Yochanan and Simeon and Eleazar, too,
and Jonathan and Judah, we will know just what to do:

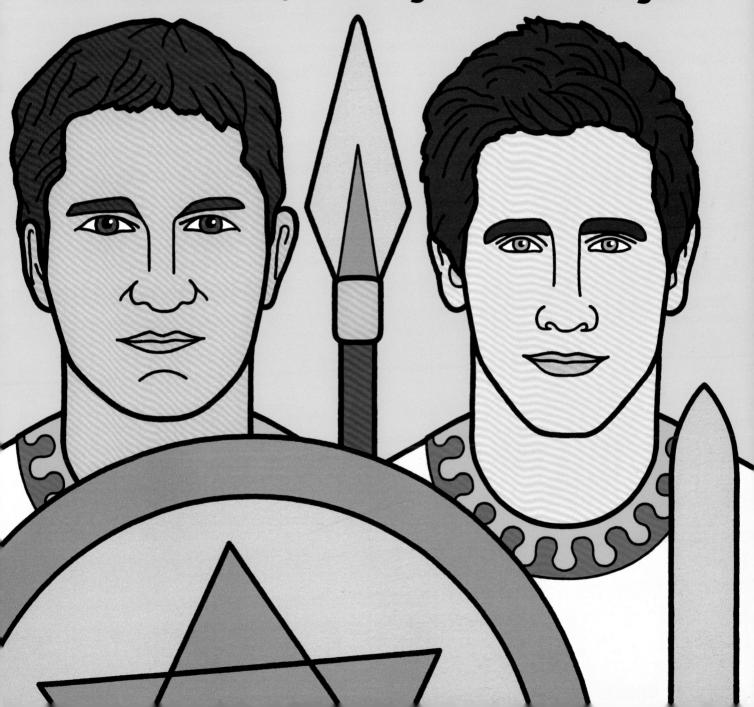

The son named Judah
was their leader,
brave and strong was he;
"hitting like a hammer"
or in Hebrew, Maccabee.

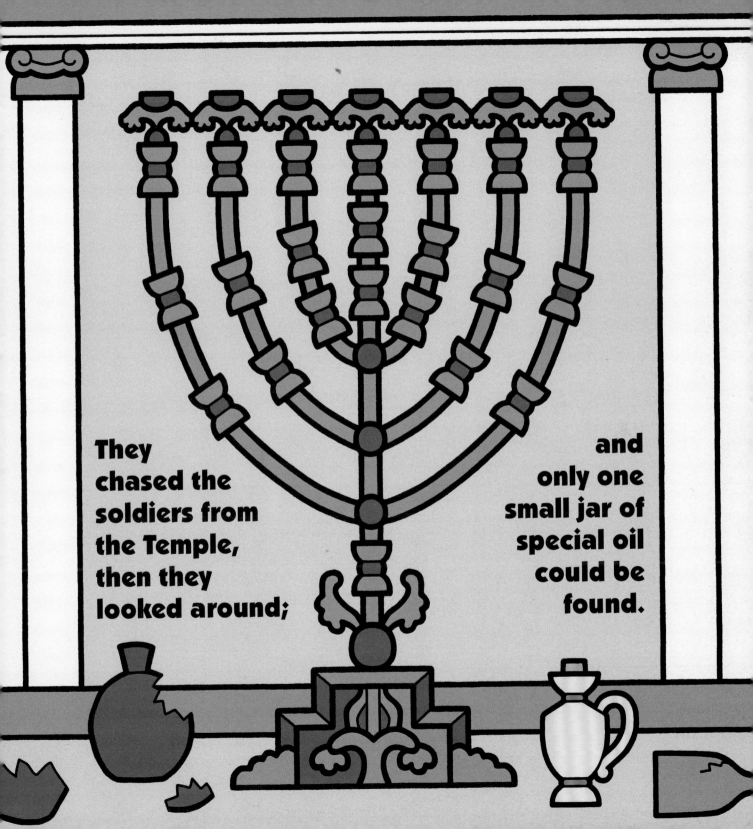

They chased the soldiers from the Temple, then they looked around;

and only one small jar of special oil could be found.

The miracle of Chanukah at this point did amaze:
that single jar of olive oil lasted
eight long days!

So this is why we light these wicks; we add one more each night.

The miracle increased each day that oil still burned bright.

1

2

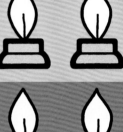

3

4

5

6

7

8

We watch the candles burning lower,
reaching their wicks' ends,
and sing together "Ma'oz Tzur"
with family and friends.

We spin the dreidel; on each side a letter in a square – spelling out the message:

A GREAT MIRACLE HAPPENED THERE!

Who gets the gelt? The letters tell us:
NUN's a neutral call.
There's half for HEY,
and SHIN must pay,
and GIMMEL gets it all!

In Israel, on a dreidel's side,
the SHIN does not appear.
The letter PEY is in its place:
**A GREAT MIRACLE
HAPPENED
*HERE.***

Israel